ADULT COLORING BOOK
CELTIC MANDALAS
—ADVANCED—

by international Celtic artist

Cari Buziak

Lil' Llama
Press

ISBN: 978-1-7386806-8-9

Celtic Mandalas - Advanced, by Cari Buziak
© 2023 Cari Buziak
Aon-Celtic.com

ADULT COLORING BOOK
CELTIC MANDALAS
—ADVANCED—

TIPS

- use a thin sheet of cardboard, poster board or bristol underneath the page you're coloring to make sure markers don't bleed through to the page underneath

- use a sharp utility or exacto knife to remove pages along the inner seam. A sheet of bristol board underneath the page being cut will ensure only one page is cut at a time.

Visit my Etsy store & website for more coloring pages and PDF eBook collections:

etsy.com/shop/AonCelticArt

Aon-Celtic.com

If you enjoyed this book, please leave a review!

Check out my other coloring books!

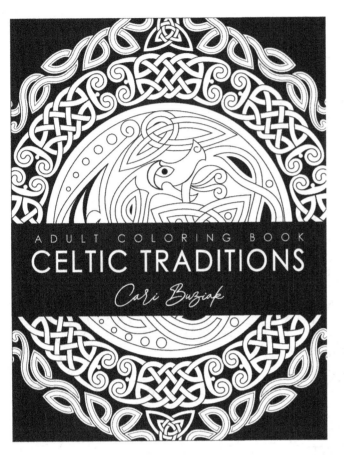

Celtic Traditions

50 pages offering a wide variety of Celtic influenced designs!

Experience this traditionally inspired art form, created in the flavour of ancient manuscripts like the Book of Kells and the Lindisfarne Gospels.

If you like variety and want a great cross-section of different Celtic topics and themes - knots, spirals, dragons, hounds, lions, birds, and more - then this is the book for you!

Celtic Patterns

50 pages of highly detailed Celtic designs!

A kaleidoscope of beautiful patterns, each featuring Celtic artwork created in a mandala style. Each design runs edge-to-edge on the page so you can color every inch! The designs in this book are highly detailed, perfect for intermediate and advanced colorists.

If you love detailed coloring and losing yourself in a design, then this book is definitely for you!

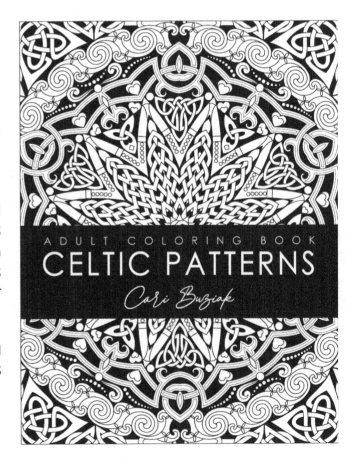

Celtic Mandalas

50 pages of inspiring Celtic mandala designs!

Two traditionally inspired art forms, blended together to create unique and beautiful pages to color. Each page features the details you love in Celtic art, in a radiating mandala styled pattern filled with knots, spirals, hearts, tendrils, curls and more.

If you love falling into the zen state of mandala coloring, then this book was made for you!

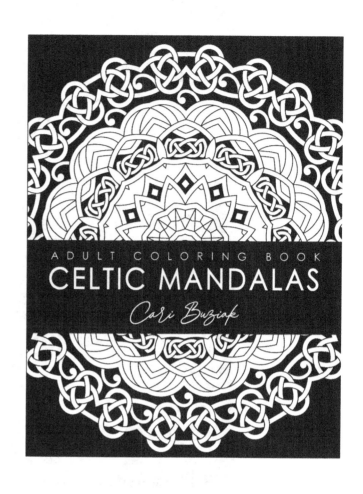

Celtic Mysteries

50 pages offering a variety of classic Celtic designs!

A fresh compilation of traditional designs, in the flavour of ancient manuscripts like the Book of Kells and the Lindisfarne Gospels.

If you're looking for an excellent cross-section of different Celtic topics and themes - knots, spirals, dragons, hounds, crosses, birds, and more - then this is the book for you!

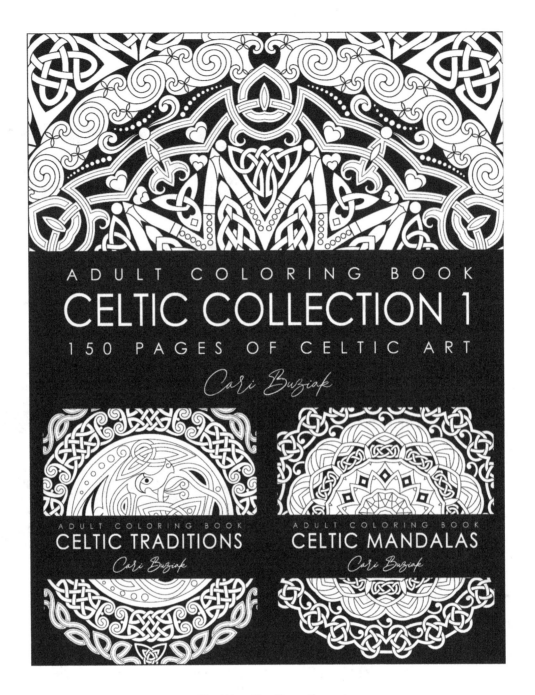

Celtic Collection I

150 pages of CELTIC COLORING in one mega-book volume!

If you love Celtic art, why choose just a single book? Get all three at once in this collected edition and save!

Celtic Traditions - a great collection of traditionally styled Celtic art - horses, hounds, peacocks, eagles, dragons, and more!

Celtic Mandalas - the perfect blend of two ancient art forms, each mandala is created to feature Celtic inspired designs.

Celtic Patterns - highly detailed pages where the artwork runs edge-to-edge to fill the entire page. Great for those days when you really want to focus and be in the "zone".

If you love all things Celtic, then this book is for you!

Welcome to my world of Coloring & Cross-Stitch!

Take this traditional hobby to the next level with these trendy patterns, designed to tickle the fancy of modern stitchers! Each chart features traditionally inspired Celtic designs jam-packed with knotwork, perfect for any room decor. With 25 patterns in varying skill levels and sizes, as well as a basic cross-stitch how-to, there's something for everyone.

https://amzn.to/45PXEt1

A bestselling Celtic coloring book on Amazon!

50 pages of Celtic mandalas, designed to delight and inspire! With detailed artwork woven with Celtic knots and patterns, each page is perfect for relaxation and meditation, with a wide array of coloring inspiration to fit every mood and engage at every skill level.

https://amzn.to/3Yl6zjB

Are you a visual learner? Do you need to see the step-by-step in action for it to "click"? Then my YouTube channel is for you! Watch how-to videos, pick up tips & tricks, and download worksheets to practice your craft.   **youtube.com/c/AonCelticArt**

Cari Buziak is a best-selling author and Celtic artist, known for her instructional books on calligraphy, cross-stitch, coloring, and Celtic art.

Visit her website **Aon-Celtic.com** to learn more!

Follow me @ aon-celtic.com!

etsy.com/shop/AonCelticArt   patreon.com/AonCelticArt

facebook.com/AonCelticArt   twitter.com/CariAon

Made in the USA
Monee, IL
14 February 2025

12270701R00063